Dunstanburgh Castle

Alastair Oswald and Jeremy Ashbee

Introduction

Silhouetted against the North Sea, the ruins of
Dunstanburgh Castle are among the most dramatic
in Britain. Begun in 1313, the castle was built
on a huge scale by Thomas, earl of Lancaster
(c.1278–1322), King Edward II's cousin and the
richest and most powerful of his barons.

If, as some historians have argued, Dunstanburgh's
origins lay in the prolonged conflict between
England and Scotland, its location is hard to explain.
The castle was too far from major roads to impede
Scottish raiders, and too remote from local villages
to offer protection easily. Recent research suggests
that the reason behind Dunstanburgh's construction
lay more in the character and political ambitions of
Lancaster, whose increasingly fierce opposition to
his king ultimately led to his execution. The castle's
site may have been partly chosen to challenge
nearby Bamburgh Castle, Edward II's key stronghold
in Northumberland. Its architectural features – in
particular the great gatehouse – were meant to
resemble and outshine the castles built in Wales by
Edward II's more respected father, Edward I.

In the 1380s, John of Gaunt (1340–99) refortified
Dunstanburgh with a new entrance and stronger
defences around the old gatehouse, converting it
into a keep. The castle was twice besieged in the
1460s during the Wars of the Roses. Thereafter, for
almost 500 years, Dunstanburgh was militarily
redundant, finally passing into state guardianship as
an ancient monument in 1929. In 1940 it was
briefly pressed into military service one last time.

*Above: Portrait of John of Gaunt,
Duke of Lancaster, from
about 1380. He began to
refortify Dunstanburgh at about
the same date*

*Facing page: Dunstanburgh Castle,
seen from Embleton Beach*

Tour

FOLLOWING THE TOUR

The tour begins at Thomas of Lancaster's gatehouse, and follows an anticlockwise route around the castle. The numbers beside the headings highlight key points on the tour, and correspond with the small plans in the margins.

From whichever direction visitors approach Dunstanburgh Castle, the ragged silhouette of the great gatehouse of Thomas of Lancaster is still, seven centuries after its construction, an awe-inspiring landmark, visible for many miles around. The gatehouse, like the castle itself, was built on a colossal scale, and designed to impress visitors, command subjects and intimidate aggressors. In recent centuries it has inspired writers and artists.

◼ THE GREAT GATEHOUSE: BARBICAN

In 1313, the first year of construction at Dunstanburgh Castle, Thomas of Lancaster ordered Master Elias the mason to build 'a gatehouse 80 feet high with a tower on either side of the gate', still a good description of the building. Even in its ruined state, the building Elias produced is one of the most imposing structures in any English castle.

In the second half of the 13th century, massive gatehouses were built in many castles belonging to earls and kings, culminating in the 1280s and 1290s with Edward I's new castles in Wales, such as Aberystwyth, Harlech and Beaumaris. All these gatehouses were designed to be three storeys high, but the stonework at Dunstanburgh shows that the frontages of its two towers continued upwards for a further two storeys. The rounded drum towers of the gatehouse differ from the square towers that predominated in castles in the north of England, and show that for this particular building the earl was influenced by fashions from further afield: he aimed to emulate the king's castles and even surpass them.

Before entering the gate-passage, a medieval visitor had to pass through an outer fortified enclosure or barbican; the low stone footings of this structure can be seen beside the path. Not enough survives to show exactly what shape it took, but it was clearly part of the original 1313 design: the bases of the drum towers still bear jagged 'toothing' where the barbican's walls were once attached. Two holes over the gateway allowed guards to observe visitors as they approached. The front of the gatehouse also shows remarkable patterns scoured by the wind into the locally quarried sandstone.

Below: View facing west, showing the footings of the barbican in front of the great gatehouse. These were uncovered during clearance works in 1929

Facing page: The Lilburn Tower, set on the highest point of the headland

⬛ GREAT GATEHOUSE: GATE-PASSAGE

The gateway, which was restored in the mid-19th century, originally had a round-headed arch. There is slight evidence that a pair of wooden gates was originally set at the outer end of the passage, but later restoration in this area has removed almost all traces. The gate-passage is roofed with a stone vault supported on chamfered ribs; the ribs at the outer end of the passage were replaced in the 19th century, but the others still bear medieval masons' marks. A portcullis hung at the inner end of the passage.

Originally, a door on each side of the passage opened into a small room for the gatekeeper and his assistants: an account of 1319 names Walter Bono in this office. The door on the left was blocked, perhaps in the late 14th century when the gatehouse was converted into a keep by walling up the main gate-passage and adding a fortified enclosure to the north side. The room on this side lies over a deep underground cellar and is no longer safe to enter. In 1543, the room was used to store lead taken from the castle's roofs. The corresponding room to the right was heated by a small fireplace and has stone cupboards in the walls and iron hooks for hanging cloaks. Its second door, leading north into the castle bailey, was formed by widening what was originally a narrow window.

Below: Reconstruction of the great gatehouse from the south. The form of the barbican is based on excavated footings and evidence in the stonework of the gatehouse itself

◼ GREAT GATEHOUSE: INNER WARD

From the inner ward, or courtyard, the bulk of the gatehouse becomes clear. It was a three-storey block and served as the principal accommodation for the earl and his household, unusual in castle gatehouses. Flanking the gate-passage are the two chimneys of the gatekeepers' lodges, probably restored in about 1930. Most remarkable are the large rectangular windows that lit the rooms on the second floor. Although the windows are damaged, enough stonework remains to show that there were three, set asymmetrically with one window in the eastern half of the building on the left, but two in the western half, on the right.

◼ GATEHOUSE

Interior: Lower Floors

Of the two doors in the rear façade, only that on the left now leads to the upper parts of the building, though the ground-floor rooms can be entered through either door. As these rooms are almost identical, the tour will follow the left-hand door and its stair, historically the principal stair in the gatehouse.

On either side of the gate-passage was a guardroom, with a latrine a few steps up inside the thickness of the outer wall. These low rooms, lit only by thin arrowslits and heated by fireplaces in their rear walls, would have been dark and

Above: The back of the ruined great gatehouse, seen from across the courtyard

Below: The gatehouse built for Thomas of Lancaster's uncle, Edward I, at Harlech in North Wales. Though similar in design, the gatehouse at Dunstanburgh was two storeys taller in places

Key to the original layout
of rooms in the 14th-century
great gatehouse

A The earl's chamber

B Guardroom, below
   the earl's hall

C Slot for the portcullis

D The level of the roof

E Entrances to latrines

F Stairs from the roof to upper
   rooms in the drum towers

comfortless, providing the bare necessities for the soldiers on duty.

A short way up the spiral stair, a landing allows a view into the first-floor room, now missing its timber floor. The tower rooms at this level were octagonal-fronted rather than round as below, and were less austere than the guardrooms; they were lit by two-light windows fitted with stone window seats. These rooms also contained fireplaces in their side walls and latrines in the thickness of the wall. The rooms were not entirely private, however: soldiers had to pass through them to reach the central room over the gate-passage. These chambers were probably used by officers in the garrison, rather than the lord and his household.

To reach the central room, visitors must now continue up to the next level, from which a modern stair runs back down to a paved floor. This room lies directly above the gate-passage and retains several features connected with defending the gate. In the front wall of the gatehouse there are two round holes at waist height: these provided a view down into the former barbican, and allowed the guards to question anyone waiting at the outer gates. In the rear wall is a recess in which the portcullis hung when raised through the slot in the floor. The square sockets in the rear wall were for timbers to secure it in position, while its ropes ran up through stone channels on to the floor above.

The room contained its own latrine in the western drum tower. It also had a small fireplace, now under the modern

CUTAWAY RECONSTRUCTION OF THE GREAT GATEHOUSE FROM THE WEST

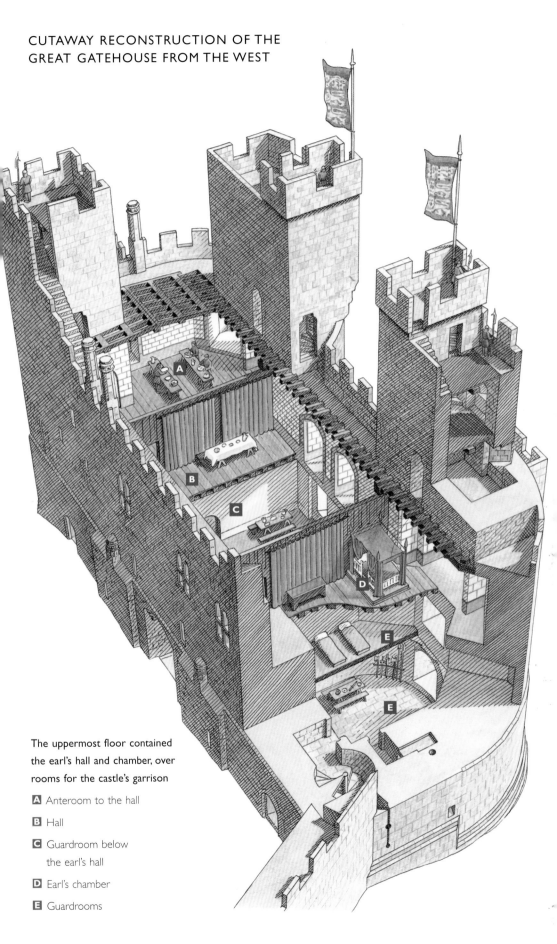

The uppermost floor contained the earl's hall and chamber, over rooms for the castle's garrison

A Anteroom to the hall

B Hall

C Guardroom below the earl's hall

D Earl's chamber

E Guardrooms

Facing page: Dunstanburgh castle seen from the south-west

access stair, with its flue built into the jamb of the window above. Originally entered through either of the adjacent rooms, this room was later provided with its own door by widening the window to the left of the portcullis, perhaps in the late 14th century when the gatehouse was converted into a keep. Presumably the function of this room completely changed at this time, with the blocking of the gate-passage below, though this is the only evident physical alteration to the building. The new door may have provided better access from a kitchen in the courtyard below.

Second Floor

The second floor, lying directly under the lead roof, contained the most important rooms in Dunstanburgh Castle: the great hall and chamber in which Lancaster and later owners planned to live. Much of the layout of this floor has been lost; the stone walls dividing up the lower levels did not continue above the first floor and at this level timber partitions must have been used. The eastern drum tower, and perhaps also its more ruined western counterpart, contained a broad arched recess around the south window, with a small fireplace in an angle. The great hall, for dining and ceremonial functions, occupied the central part of this floor, entered from the spiral stair through an imposing arched doorway. The corresponding western stair gave access only to a narrow dog-leg passageway, and was evidently a more private entrance, appropriate for the earl's chamber, the inner sanctum reserved for the earl and his intimates. On his only known visit to Dunstanburgh in 1319, Thomas of Lancaster presumably slept in this room at the west end.

Roofs and Turrets

Returning to the eastern spiral stair, it is possible to climb higher past a door that once led on to the former low-pitched lead roof and the battlements, and up through a broken 'umbrella vault' that once capped the stair turret. The top of the stair, 15.5m above the ground, offers magnificent views over the castle and surrounding countryside (see opposite).

This is also the best place to appreciate Master Elias's ambitious design for the gatehouse, whose highest point was originally 24m above the ground. Uniquely at Dunstanburgh, the fronts of the two drum towers stretched upwards above the main roof for a further two storeys. Soldiers manning the battlements could shelter from the weather in small garret rooms inside the towers; parts of the walls and a door still survive in the eastern tower.

Doors in the sides of the towers also gave access by spiral staircases to more rooms immediately above these garrets, and higher still, to the roofs of the drum towers. The towers

Floor plans of the gatehouse

Second floor

First floor

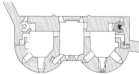

Ground floor

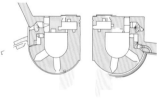

1313–c.1325
1372–83
pale shade indicates footings

0   10m
0   30ft

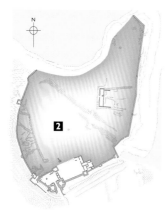

also contained small rectangular turrets whose battlements were slightly higher than the main drums. This created a striking outline of towers increasing in height towards the centre of the building. Master Elias's design provided more lookouts above the rear spiral stairs, reached by narrow stairs from the main battlements. With commanding views all round, the castle's watchmen had ample opportunity to observe anyone approaching long before they came into close range.

Looking out to sea along the castle's southern wall, it is noticeable that the wall is fronted by a dry moat, dug down to the surface of the basalt bedrock. Much of the depth of the moat is created by an earthen bank outside it, whose rear edge is retained by a drystone wall. This bank pre-dates medieval strip fields, which are visible as low ridges on the gentle slope to the south; these fields in turn pre-date the construction of the castle. The bank is now thought to represent the partially levelled rampart of an Iron Age promontory fort, probably dating to about the third century BC. In designing his castle, Lancaster appears to have made use of the Iron Age bank to deepen the dry moat.

2 BAILEY

From the courtyard, the gateway on the right, believed to have been narrowed to its present width in the 16th century, leads into the wide open space of the castle's outer bailey. Both before the castle's construction and after its abandonment, this area was under arable cultivation. Today, the grass is deliberately left long and rough to provide a habitat for nesting sea birds, but in winter, when the grass is shorter, traces of the strip fields are still visible.

Some historians have inferred that the vast space of the interior was designed to hold the army of soldiers and retainers who would have accompanied a nobleman of Lancaster's status. Others have imagined the castle bustling with hundreds of local people and all their livestock, taking

Right: Sheep grazing in the bailey before the excavation of John of Gaunt's mantlet

The Medieval Harbour

Archaeologists have discovered the remains of a harbour, which may explain the curious position of the castle gatehouse

Above: Dunstanburgh Castle painted by J M W Turner in about 1828
Below: Basalt boulders, showing the edge of a medieval jetty

Today, Lancaster's great gatehouse dominates the coastal path from Craster, 1¼ miles to the south. Yet when the castle was built in 1313, arable fields stretched right to the sea edge, while the medieval site of 'Craucester' lay further inland than the modern village (see map, page 33). Embleton, the chief settlement of the barony lay nearly 2 miles to the north-west, and the main approach to the castle by land was from this direction. So why did Dunstanburgh's gatehouse face south-east, away from the approach and the settlement?

Archaeologists have recently made a discovery which may help to explain this. In 2003, on the foreshore at the foot of the castle outcrop, they recognised among the sharp, slippery basalt boulders the foundations of a 75m-long stone jetty. This jetty would have been invaluable for transporting materials to the building site, but in 1319 accounts also mention oars for the 'earl's boat', and replacement boats appear in later documents.

The fact that Lancaster's great gatehouse faces towards the end of the jetty is probably no accident. A noble visitor approaching by sea would have been overawed by the scale of the castle, but the full impact of the symmetrical towers of the great gatehouse would have been saved until the moment of disembarkation. It seems likely that Lancaster was inspired by royal castles in Wales and the Tower of London, at which the lord and important guests could arrive by water.

refuge from rampaging Scots. Engaging though these images are, it seems unlikely that the castle's interior was often much busier than it is today. Just like the builders of the Iron Age fort, Thomas of Lancaster took advantage of the natural topography by building his rampart across the narrow neck of the promontory, and the huge size of the bailey (4 hectares) was a by-product of his pragmatic approach.

◼ CONSTABLE'S TOWER

The Constable's Tower stands ahead along the south wall, with later accommodation built against its rear side. These lodgings were not part of the original design, but had been added by 1351, when an account mentions repairs to the roofs of 'the constable's hall and chamber'. Some of the foundations visible today were exposed between 1930 and 1931, but a geophysical survey carried out in 1989 suggests that the remains of more buildings lie concealed beneath the turf.

The tower was part of the original design for Thomas of Lancaster and always provided accommodation. On its upper floors the windows have adjacent stone seats, similar to those in the great gatehouse, suggesting that even in the earliest days, the rooms were more comfortable than basic guardrooms. The constable of Dunstanburgh was an important figure locally, entrusted with the command of the castle when the earl was elsewhere, and with safeguarding his surrounding lands. Thomas of Lancaster is thought to have visited his stronghold only once, and John of Gaunt did not visit often. In their absence, the constables exercised their authority.

Below: Adjoining the Constable's Tower are the ruins of a large house, probably the 'constable's hall and chamber' mentioned in an account of 1351

◢ EGYNCLEUGH TOWER

Further down the curtain wall is Egyncleugh Tower, whose name means 'eagle's ravine' in local dialect. Today, the ravine goes by the name of Queen Margaret's Cove, referring to the escape by Queen Margaret of Anjou (1430–82) after her supposed landing here in October 1462, during the Wars of the Roses. In reality, this tale is a misleading piece of Victorian romanticism, for Queen Margaret landed not at Dunstanburgh but at Bamburgh, and in any event she was speedily repulsed.

Egyncleugh Tower comprised a narrow gateway on the ground floor with lodgings above it, which, like the Constable's Tower, evidently housed an important official. Most of the tower's architectural details are best seen from outside the curtain wall after leaving the castle. The dry moat was cut deep into the bedrock at this point and was originally crossed by a drawbridge. The gate, too narrow to allow carts to pass and too low for horsemen, may have been the point at which local people were allowed to enter the castle's interior, keeping them well away from the lord's lodgings in the great gatehouse. Alternatively it may have been a private entrance for the constable.

◢ EAST WALL

Descending the steps, the path passes a small postern gate, known to have been added in the 1450s, which gave access to the foreshore. Beyond this, the wall is not built of squared sandstone blocks, but of small lumps of limestone, another

Above: As a precaution against violent raids from Scotland, the tenants of the barony of Embleton occasionally took shelter inside the castle with their property and livestock

Below: The Egyncleugh Tower contained a narrow gateway below two storeys of residential rooms. The fragment of the front wall contains traces of a rectangular recess which housed the drawbridge when raised. Immune to the picturesque qualities of Queen Margaret's Cove, the more practical medieval builders sited the latrines over the cliff edge

Above: Aerial view of Dunstanburgh Castle from the north-east, across the outer ward. The remains of the barn and it yard are visible as a raised rectangle in the grass

local stone. Joints along the wall show that it was built in sections, either by different gangs of workers or in stages, perhaps over the course of several years. It is possible that the eastern wall of the castle was built by the inhabitants of Embleton as part of their duty to their lord, using stone that was available to them closer to the village. Perhaps Lancaster allowed the villagers to provide themselves with the three latrines sited at intervals along the wall.

The original walk along the top of the wall, sheltered behind a parapet, can be seen in several places; it was only 3.3m above the external ground surface. At some point, the whole wall was raised using basalt boulders taken from the foreshore. This may suggest a rapid response to some specific crisis, perhaps during the Wars of the Roses, when naval landings posed a greater threat than they had when the castle was first built.

6 BARN

On the left lie the overgrown foundations of a rectangular building with an attached yard, once surrounded by a drystone wall that has long since tumbled down. The building has usually been identified as the 'grange', or barn, mentioned in several 15th-century documents. Excavations in 1930 to 1931 were unable to prove the theory, but its size and plan are certainly consistent with a barn. The poor quality of the walling would be typical of the infilling normally used between the major structural elements of a timber-framed building.

7 GULL CRAG

Near the far end of the east wall is another gateway, which gives access to the rocky outcrop known as Castle Point. This is a puzzling location for a gate, although the deep water beneath Gull Crag – as the 30m cliff that forms the northern defence of the castle is known – may have been as attractive to fishermen in the Middle Ages as it is today. Perhaps the real reason for the gate's existence lies in the fact that the castle's main harbour to the south, at Nova Scotia beach, was inaccessible without leaving the safety of the outer defences. In the event of a siege, the deep water below Gull Crag would have allowed a boat to come within easy swimming distance of the shore, even if the sea was too rough to allow it to land on the rocky foreshore. If the sea is stormy, this part of the castle is regularly soaked by the spray surging up a natural cavity in the basalt, called Rumbling Churn. It is unclear whether the castle wall ever extended along the edge of Gull Crag, but if so, it was certainly not a major defensive work. There was no need for it: as the antiquarian Cadwallader Bates observed in 1891, the cliffs themselves formed the northern rampart of the castle.

Below: The cliffs of Gull Crag are 30m high in places, leaving no need for a high curtain wall to defend the north side of the castle

Above: The Lilburn Tower dominates
Embleton beach and the site
of the north mere
Below: The Lilburn Tower from the
south-east

⑧ LILBURN TOWER

Rising above the western end of the cliff is the Lilburn Tower,
named after John de Lilburn, who became constable in 1322,
after Thomas of Lancaster's execution. Based on its name, it
has been suggested that the tower may actually have been
built by Lilburn in the 1320s. The design and quality of work,
however, suggest that it was part of Lancaster's original design,
though Lilburn may have finished the building after Lancaster's
death. Like the Constable's Tower and Egyncleugh Tower, this
was probably the residence of an important official, for it too
was provided with fine windows and window seats. Common
soldiers may have lodged on the ground floor, which had no
access to the rooms above. From the footpath far below, two
projecting latrines are prominently visible on the exterior, their
positions carefully staggered with the outlet of the upper
latrine well away from the lower.

The high ground on which the Lilburn Tower was built
commands an excellent view northwards towards the golden
sweep of Embleton beach. In the early years of the Second
World War, this beach was recognised as a potential site for a
seaborne invasion launched from Norway, and this threat
played its own part in Dunstanburgh's history (see pages
38–9). On a clear day, the tower of the royal stronghold at
Bamburgh can also be seen, nearly ten miles north along the
coast. It is no accident that Lancaster chose this position for
such a tall, elegant and imposing building as the Lilburn Tower,
whose height has often led people to interpret it as
a watchtower. Bamburgh was Dunstanburgh's 'rival' and
Lancaster was evidently exploiting the natural advantages

of the setting with a striking piece of architecture which noble visitors, and perhaps the garrison of Bamburgh, would have recognised as a symbolic challenge to the authority of Edward II.

⑨ WEST WALL

The castle's western wall is shown almost intact in Francis Place's engraving of 1678 (see pages 36–7); most of the good quality sandstone facing blocks have since been taken away for reuse. A shapeless lump of stonework, known locally as Huggam's House (for unknown reasons), is all that survives of a minor tower that strengthened an angle in the wall. To the left is a grassy bank, running between the Lilburn Tower and the rear of Lancaster's great gatehouse. Despite excavations in 1930 to 1931, the function of this earthwork remains uncertain. Slight traces on the ground surface suggest that the bank may have enclosed several buildings, a pattern similar to the arrangement behind the castle's southern wall.

⑩ JOHN OF GAUNT'S GATEHOUSE

Following the remains of the curtain wall around the circuit leads to the low stonework of a gatehouse overlooking the approach from Embleton. This gate was begun in July 1383 on the orders of the duke of Lancaster, John of Gaunt (1340–99), and was the last in a series of works that completely changed the way in which Dunstanburgh Castle operated. It is not certain what was here beforehand: Thomas of Lancaster's curtain wall turned an angle at this point and a tower and a gate probably stood here. Certainly the new structure, built by the local mason Henry Holme, reused materials salvaged

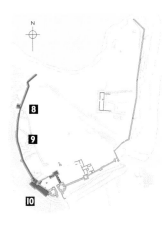

Below left: The antiquarian Cadwallader Bates wrote in 1891, 'You almost expect to be challenged by the basalt giants that are drawn up like so many warders round the base of the stately Lilburn Tower'

Below right: The remains of John of Gaunt's gatehouse, built in 1383, replacing Thomas of Lancaster's great gatehouse as the main entrance

from an 'old gatehouse'. A modest two- or three-storey building, Gaunt's new gatehouse contained a porter's lodge north of the gate-passage. It had a portcullis, the slot for which can still be seen in the sides of the gate-passage, together with settings for the timber gates. Outside, the path turned sharply left along a terrace, and here a sequence of two barbicans protected the final approach, probably incorporating a drawbridge between the two.

⑪ MANTLET

The new gate led into the expanse of the castle's interior. Three years previously, however, Gaunt had sealed off a small area around Thomas of Lancaster's gatehouse. The stone wall or mantlet between the old and new gatehouses is part of this alteration, ordered in October 1380 from the celebrated northern master mason John Lewyn. When first built, this mantlet was simply an enclosing wall of dressed stone, 20ft (6m) high to the battlements and 4ft (1.2m) thick. It originally contained a gateway in its north wall, in a line directly between the gate-passage of the original gatehouse and the Lilburn Tower. Changes in the stone coursing of the wall show where this opening was almost immediately blocked with new stonework. The mantlet originally did little more than give the lord and his household in the gatehouse some privacy from the castle's other occupants in the bailey.

At the left-hand (north-east) end of the wall stands the base of a projecting rectangular tower. This was added to the mantlet as a second phase, between December 1381 and September 1382, and was the work of Henry Holme, who had replaced Lewyn as mason at Dunstanburgh in 1381. Holme's commission was to create a new 'gatehouse with a vault, a portcullis and a spiral stair', the vault and stair being located inside the new corner tower. The former gate in the north wall was probably walled up at this time, so when access through Thomas of Lancaster's gatehouse was eventually blocked, this new gate in the east wall of the mantlet became the main entrance into the inner part of the castle.

⑫ INNER WARD

This gateway leads into the courtyard, or inner ward, created by John of Gaunt. The opening is now remarkably narrow and low, suitable for foot traffic but impassable for vehicles or those on horseback. In 1538, however, the gateway was still 'three yards [2.75m] broad' as originally built, and it must have been made smaller at a later date, perhaps during the brief occupancy of Alice Craster between 1594 and 1597 (see page 35).

When adding this new gate between 1381 and 1382, Holme also built 'six houses with six vaults, six chimneys and windows'. Remains of these buildings can be seen as low walls around the courtyard. One of the houses served as an

Development of the mantlet and John of Gaunt's gatehouse

Mantlet begun October 1380

Service buildings and vaulted gatehouse begun December 1381

New gatehouse and barbican begun July 1383

0 ——————— 50m
0 ——————— 50yds

antechamber to the great gatehouse door, replacing an
earlier building on the same site, and on the north side was
a bakehouse with its oven. There would also have been a
kitchen to serve the old gatehouse, probably close to the
castle's well: a 'kitchen tower' was described in the early 15th
century as newly built. With these ancillary buildings, the old
gatehouse and its new courtyard had become a self-contained
residence, fit for the greatest lord and strong enough to hold
out against attack.

Above: The medieval meres
below the castle occasionally flood,
even today
Below: Photograph of the great
gatehouse in 1884, showing the
remains of two stone walls
blocking the entrance. The wall
at the far end may date to the
late 14th century

FROM GATEHOUSE TO KEEP

Before returning through the gate-passage to leave the castle,
it is useful to look again at the rear of the gatehouse, as
massive as any castle keep. Fifteenth-century documents show
that this is exactly what it had become, calling it 'the tower
called le dungeoun' (at the time this meant not a prison but
the residence of a lord). It has usually been assumed that John
of Gaunt walled up the gate-passage in the 1380s, and in
16th-century surveys of Dunstanburgh, this building is not
listed among the castle's gates. Certainly stone walls across the
former gate-passage can be seen in late 18th-century paintings
by J M W Turner and in drawings and photographs of the
19th century; and by the late 19th century there were walls
at both ends of the passage. They have been cleared away
during more recent restorations and, for the first time since
the 14th century, the outward view is clear of obstruction
down to the medieval harbour and the sea beyond.

The Meres

Recent research has shown that the castle was isolated by a series of freshwater meres, a piece of medieval landscape design on a grand scale

Looking inland from just beyond the Lilburn Tower, a stretch of moat 101m long (or exactly 20 perches, as specified in the accounts of 1313), can be seen. It usually retains a pool of water, and though this appears shallow, the medieval accounts specify the depth of the ditch as 18ft (5.5m).

Until recently, the purpose of this isolated moat was not fully understood. English Heritage's archaeological survey in 2003, however, showed that its northern end connected with the northernmost of three freshwater lakes or meres, forming a continuous stretch of water. Following the crest along the inner edges of the meres was an earthen bank, probably topped by a timber palisade, which formed an outer perimeter for the castle. The natural causeway that dammed the north mere from the sea was blocked by a stone-faced earthwork which ran from near the Lilburn Tower down to the edge of the mere.

At its southern end, the moat ended at another causeway, which divided it from the second of the three meres. To keep the meres full, water from a spring further inland was channelled to this point, where it was controlled using a system of sluices and overflow channels. The same water supply fed a series of small outlying fish ponds, where freshwater fish were

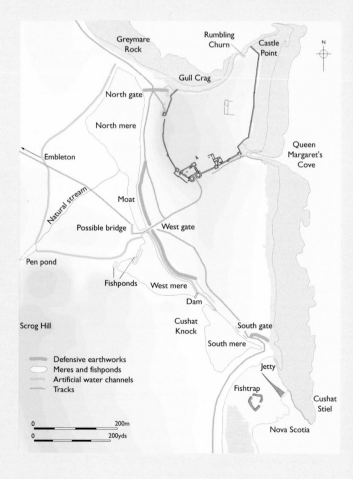

Right: Map showing the medieval meres around Dunstanburgh Castle. The effect on a visitor, approaching the castle for the first time, would have been dramatic

bred and kept for the occupants of the castle. The principal
medieval route from Embleton, parts of which survive as a farm
track, crossed the causeway at this point, and it is likely that a
gatehouse stood here, although little trace of it survives.
Important visitors who did not arrive by sea would have
followed this route. Further south was the third mere, now an
area of marshy ground, once thought to be the medieval harbour.

Today it is difficult to imagine how spectacular the approach
from Embleton must have been. At the foot of the Lilburn
Tower, natural rock pillars were deliberately preserved intact by
the builders, with the tower growing out of them. The Lilburn
Tower, reflected in the shallow water of the northernmost
mere, would have been an awe-inspiring and beautiful sight,
dominating the entire approach. The meres contributed to the
defences of the outermost perimeter and served as a larder for
fish and wild birds, but they were also partly ornamental, a piece
of medieval landscape design on a grand scale. The same is true
of other large medieval meres, such as those at Kenilworth
Castle in Warwickshire and Framlingham Castle in Suffolk. The
indirect approach would have meant that visitors were
unprepared, when they eventually turned to face the great
gatehouse, for the immense size and extraordinary design of
this architectural masterpiece. This dramatic conclusion was
undoubtedly part of Lancaster's intention in designing a
landscape setting for his showpiece.

*Top: Reconstruction of
Dunstanburgh Castle from the north
in about 1325, showing the meres
that ran around the western side,
turning the castle into an island*
Above: *Medieval manuscript showing
the mythical 'Joyous Garde', the
castle of Sir Launcelot, with a mere
before a great gatehouse, just as at
the real Dunstanburgh Castle*

History

Begun on the grandest possible scale in 1313 by
Edward II's over-mighty subject Thomas, earl of
Lancaster, Dunstanburgh was much altered by
John of Gaunt in the 1380s. Though it played
a brief role in the Wars of the Roses, it ceased
to have any military purpose soon afterwards,
and fell increasingly into decay.

BEFORE THE CASTLE

The history of Dunstanburgh Castle itself begins in 1313. Archaeologists have long speculated, however, about the existence of a much earlier settlement on the promontory occupied by the castle. Scraps of prehistoric and Roman pottery were unearthed here during restoration work by the Ministry of Works in the 1920s, and the discovery of a Roman brooch at the foot of the eastern wall prompted exploratory excavations near the tip of the headland between 1930 and 1931. These revealed an Iron Age hearth, perhaps dating to the first century BC, and a hearth associated with Roman pottery dating to the second century AD. A box containing artefacts found in the 1920s was rediscovered in 2005, hidden away in the locked room on the west side of the gate-passage. The artefacts included a number of small millstones, also of Iron Age date.

English Heritage's archaeological survey in 2003 helped to put the discoveries of the 1920s into context. A broad, low earthen bank, which effectively forms the edge of the dry moat in front of the castle's southern wall, was shown to be of an earlier date than the evidence of medieval ploughing, which itself pre-dates the construction of the castle wall. An ancient earthwork of this size and form – presumably narrower and higher before the ploughing – may well be the rampart of an Iron Age promontory fort, a variant of the more common hillfort. Excavation of similar forts further inland suggests that many were constructed in the third century BC; occupation often continued well after the Roman military campaign of AD 79, when the armies of Agricola, the Roman governor of Britain, reached the Scottish highlands.

Until recently, it was believed that the name Dunstanburgh was a 14th-century invention, deliberately contrived by Thomas of Lancaster to sound like Bamburgh. The suffix 'burgh', which means fortification in Old English, occurs in different forms in many medieval place names, such as Edinburgh, Scarborough and Salisbury. The ancient earthwork may therefore lie behind the 'burgh' element of Dunstanburgh's name. But by 1313, when the promontory was chosen as the site of the new castle, the headland, along with much of the surrounding land, had apparently been under arable cultivation for hundreds of years.

THOMAS, EARL OF LANCASTER AND HIS CASTLE

In 1298 Thomas, earl of Lancaster (c.1278–1322), inherited the barony of Embleton from his father, Edmund 'Crouchback' (1245–96), younger brother of King Edward I. Previous lords of Embleton included the famous rebel Simon de Montfort, earl of Leicester (1208–65), on whose career Thomas may have modelled his own. For over a decade, Lancaster did little with his Northumberland possessions, beyond imposing a

Facing page: Detail from an illuminated manuscript of the mid-14th century, showing Thomas, earl of Lancaster and St George. After his execution in 1322, Thomas was revered by many as a saint

protégé, Peter de Dene, as priest of Embleton church over the rightful claimant from Merton College, Oxford. Changing circumstances after 1312, however, made it prudent for him to provide himself with a refuge in his northernmost estate, especially following his part in the death of Edward II's favourite and alleged lover, Piers Gaveston.

Thomas of Lancaster became prominent in opposition to the royal government, particularly the influence at court of the outspoken Gaveston. Possibly the seeds of Lancaster's dispute with his cousin Edward II lay in their childhood: it has been suggested that the warlike King Edward I had preferred Lancaster's character to that of his own son Edward, the future king. In April 1312, Lancaster and other earls led an army against Gaveston, who had returned from banishment, forcing his surrender at Scarborough Castle. While being escorted to London under safe conduct, Gaveston was seized by Lancaster's ally, the earl of Warwick, and beheaded on Lancaster's land. Lancaster, to whom Gaveston's severed head was presented, had been among the earls who condemned Gaveston to death, an act for which contemporaries believed that Edward II later took revenge.

Though Lancaster was formally pardoned for his part in Gaveston's death a few months afterwards, it was in the tense aftermath of these events that work began at Dunstanburgh. In a time of increasing danger from Scotland, it would be only sensible for a landowner like Lancaster to protect his most vulnerable estate with a castle, though this seems not to have been his prime motive. It is more likely that he saw Dunstanburgh as a place of refuge for himself, as far away from his English enemies as he could manage. What he eventually created there, however, was inspired as much by aesthetics and perhaps even by mythology as any practical concern for defence.

The construction of the castle began in the spring of 1313, and is amply documented in its earliest phases. In the first year, several northern abbeys and friendly individuals donated oxen and carthorses (one of which was stolen by Scottish raiders). Lancaster recruited teams of quarrymen, ditchers to excavate the western moat and the channels for the meres, and various other labourers, for whom a wooden lodge was built on the site. Iron was purchased to make crowbars, hammers and picks; three limekilns fired by coal from Newcastle were built to provide the mortar; and Scandinavian boards were bought to make doors and windows. The accounts also speak of wooden scaffolding, lead for gutters and bags for carrying materials. In the first year, Lancaster also made a contract with 'Master Elias the mason' to build the gatehouse for £224 in silver, to be paid in instalments.

Unfortunately the later progress of the works is less well understood. They seem not to have been disrupted by Scottish incursions, not even after the calamitous English defeat at Bannockburn in June 1314, from which Lancaster absented himself. Politically, Lancaster's attentions were increasingly concentrated elsewhere in trying to control Edward II's government, although from 1317 he began to recruit prominent (and unruly) Northumberland knights into his retinue. Thomas received a licence to crenellate the new castle in August 1315 (representing official royal recognition of a non-royal castle), and most of the works were probably finished by March 1319, when Robert de Binchester was appointed as its first constable. In August of that year,

Left: *Victorian illustration showing the head of Piers Gaveston being presented to the earls of Warwick, Lancaster and Hereford in April 1312*

Meanings and Myths of Dunstanburgh

In building
Dunstanburgh,
Lancaster may have
been motivated
by an interest in
Arthurian legend,
and his dramatic
castle certainly
inspired later myths

If Dunstanburgh Castle looks as though it was built as an extravagant theatrical display, this may not be far from reality. Thomas of Lancaster lavished money on Dunstanburgh Castle's design out of all proportion to its military value and surrounded it with artificial meres, effectively turning it into an island. Both its architecture and setting may have been influenced more by symbolism and mythology than by practicalities.

Some scholars believe that the watery landscapes created by Lancaster and other noblemen may have reflected ideas in contemporary literature, such as Avalon, the island on which King Arthur was buried, or Sir Launcelot's castle, Joyous Garde (see page 23). During the height of its popularity among the English aristocracy from the 13th to the 16th centuries, Arthurian mythology was politically potent. Several members of the royal family took an interest in the legends: Edward I, for example, ordered the construction of a round table at Winchester. There is evidence that Thomas of Lancaster, too, was interested in Arthur: in his treacherous dealings with the Scots, he apparently used the pseudonym 'King Arthur', and at his trial in 1322 he was mockingly saluted as 'O King Arthur, most dreadful'. It is intriguing to speculate if in building Dunstanburgh, Lancaster was motivated by an interest in Arthurian legend and even perhaps in portraying himself as the mythical king.

Lancaster's dramatic castle certainly inspired later myths, one of which has strong Arthurian overtones. First recorded in 1808, it tells the story of a knight, Guy the Seeker, who seeks shelter at the castle. Presented by a wizard with a choice of magical tools – a sword or Merlin's horn – to rescue a lady held captive in a crystal coffin, Sir Guy makes the wrong choice, and is cast outside the castle walls again. He is said to wander there to this day, seeking a way back inside.

Below left: The round table in the great hall of Winchester Castle, made in the late 13th century probably for Edward I, Thomas of Lancaster's uncle

Below right: Like Dunstanburgh, Tintagel in Cornwall had ancient remains, but on account of its mythical associations with King Arthur, was converted into a castle in the Middle Ages

Left: Mid-14th-century manuscript illustration of the beheading of Thomas of Lancaster in 1322. Lancaster was unofficially venerated as a victim of royal murder, like his namesake St Thomas Becket

Lancaster probably stayed at Dunstanburgh on his way to join the English siege of Berwick-upon-Tweed, which the Scots had captured the previous year: an account mentions a payment to 'six cart-drivers from Dunstanburgh travelling with three wagons to Scotland with the lord'. If he did indeed use Dunstanburgh as a base before the siege of Berwick – which failed partly as a result of his quarrelling with the other commanders – this was the only time Lancaster saw his new castle.

In March 1322, however, as a baronial revolt led by Lancaster against Edward II and his favourites (this time the elder and younger Hugh Despenser) began to collapse, Dunstanburgh seemed the safest place for the earl and his followers to escape from the king's anger. They held a council of war in the Blackfriars at Pontefract in West Yorkshire, and decided that 'by common assent, they should all go to the castle of Dunstanburgh, which pertained to the earldom of Lancaster, and abide there till the king had forgiven him'. Lancaster initially refused, arguing that to go north would fuel rumours that he was conspiring with Robert the Bruce of Scotland, as indeed he was. But he was overruled, and it was while making for Dunstanburgh that on 16 March his dwindling army was intercepted at Boroughbridge in North Yorkshire and defeated by a royalist force. Lancaster was captured alive and, after a humiliating trial, was beheaded at Pontefract. Dunstanburgh Castle passed into the hands of the victorious king.

THE CASTLE AFTER THOMAS OF LANCASTER

Though affairs of England rather than Scotland had caused Lancaster to build Dunstanburgh Castle, Edward II considered it potentially important for border security and took care that it remained in good order. Two days after Lancaster's execution,

Above: Mid-14th-century manuscript illustration of a woman carrying a heavy sack. An account of 1351 contains a rare mention of a 'handmaid', helping labourers to repair the gatehouse and Lilburn Tower

the Newcastle merchant Richard de Emeldon (Embleton) was entrusted with the castle 'by reason of the disturbed state of the realm and the invasion of the Scots', to hold it with a garrison of 40 foot soldiers and 40 hobelars (lightly armed cavalry). The castle's buildings were completed around this time. The naming of the Lilburn Tower after John de Lilburn, joint constable between September 1322 and the summer of 1323, suggests that this tower was finished during his term of office, while his successor, Roger Heron, was ordered to repair 'an ancient hall in the castle or another house there'.

By April 1326, Dunstanburgh was in the hands of Earl Thomas's younger brother, Henry (c.1280–1345), who had been reacquiring the territories and titles of his brother. Scottish invasions, which posed a constant threat during the 1330s, became acute in the following decade after David II of Scotland (1329–71) returned from France in 1341, and only ended with the Scottish defeat at Neville's Cross, north of Durham, in October 1346. In the early 1350s, an account recorded that property had been 'preserved in the castle from Scottish attack', presumably the goods of local people sheltering inside the fortress. Though damaged by the weather rather than warfare, the 30-year-old castle needed heavy repairs, especially the barn and constable's house, the Lilburn Tower and the high turrets of the great gatehouse.

JOHN OF GAUNT (1340–99)

In 1362, Dunstanburgh Castle, now part of a duchy rather than an earldom, came into the possession of one of the greatest dukes of Lancaster, John of Gaunt, Edward III's third son. Gaunt inherited the title and lands through his first wife, Blanche, granddaughter of Henry of Lancaster. Though initially he had little interest in the north of England, he ordered occasional repairs to Dunstanburgh Castle. In 1379 he became lieutenant in the Scottish marches, responsible for the security of the border. A visit to Northumberland in October 1380 evidently brought home to him several shortcomings in the design of Dunstanburgh Castle, and over the next three years its layout was completely transformed.

Gaunt's first new building was simply a wall or mantlet, 6m high and 1.3m thick, running around the north side of the gatehouse. This separated his apartments in the gatehouse from the rest of the bailey, which was largely given over to the business of the estate, though a gate through the north wall connected the two areas. During the peasants' revolt of June 1381, however, Gaunt was a prime target for the rebels' hostility. He sought and was denied shelter in Alnwick Castle by the earl of Northumberland, as he feared that Dunstanburgh would not be strong enough. This confirmed Gaunt's need for a genuine stronghold of his own. He therefore ordered that the mantlet should be strengthened

Sir John de Lilburn

Sir John de Lilburn, constable of Dunstanburgh from September 1322 to the summer of 1323, gave his name to the Lilburn Tower. His career was notable for violence, banditry and political betrayal

A minor Northumberland landowner, Lilburn was among those pardoned in 1313 for 'the capture, detention or death' of Piers Gaveston, and became a knight of the royal household. Like numerous similar 'schavaldours' (a dialect term for leaders of armed gangs), Lilburn was effectively above the law. In August 1315, he ambushed and tried to murder a royal judge at Alnwick to avenge the hanging of some alleged traitors at Berwick. In 1316, he incurred the enmity of another royal retainer, Roger Mauduit, for ransoming Mauduit's three Scottish prisoners without permission and keeping the money for himself. Lilburn may also have participated in September 1317 in the infamous highway robbery and abduction of two cardinals and the bishop-elect of Durham just south of that city; and the following month he seized Knaresborough Castle in Yorkshire from a royal favourite, Roger Damory. Soon afterwards Lilburn was recruited, like other local schavaldours, into the anti-royal faction of Thomas of Lancaster. He deserted Lancaster, however, and rejoined Edward II's household before the battle of Boroughbridge in March 1322, fighting in the royalist army against his former patron.

Lilburn's term as constable of Dunstanburgh, partnered by his old enemy Roger Mauduit, was short-lived, though the Lilburn Tower may have been finished during this time. He never completely abandoned his old ways: as late as 1327, the year in which he also became sheriff of Northumberland, he is recorded as stealing £100-worth of goods from the parson of Embleton.

Below: Fourteenth-century manuscript showing the kind of violence for which Sir John de Lilburn and his fellow 'schavaldours' were feared in Northumberland

with a new corner tower and gateway from the main bailey, and also provided new service buildings in the courtyard. The final development, in 1383, was to build a new entrance into the main bailey from outside the castle, protected by barbicans and a drawbridge. This new gate became the principal entrance into the castle; Lancaster's gate seems to have been blocked. Significantly, the great gatehouse was thereafter called 'donjon', the lord's tower. The building had always been the principal residential building in the castle, but henceforth this was supposed to be its only function: no longer a gatehouse, it had become the keep.

Above: Seal of John of Gaunt, king of Castile and León and duke of Lancaster
Below: *Bread oven built in the inner ward of Dunstanburgh Castle, probably in the time of John of Gaunt*

THE 15TH CENTURY AND THE WARS OF THE ROSES

In 1399, John of Gaunt's son claimed the throne as King Henry IV (1399–1413), and the duchy of Lancaster was annexed to the Crown. Numerous accounts survive from the reign of Henry VI (1422–61), showing that various buildings in Dunstanburgh Castle were repaired, furnished and rebuilt during this time. These included the seaward curtain wall, stables and barns, the royal chapel (whose location has not yet been identified), the chamber of the auditor and receiver of Dunstanburgh and the royal apartments in the former gatehouse (which had an 'alarm bell' on its roof). The fortifications were also sporadically repaired and in the late 1450s a 'tower at the castle entrance' was rebuilt, perhaps an outwork to John of Gaunt's gate. The accounts also contain many details about the peacetime relationship between Dunstanburgh Castle and its estate. From the earliest days of

the castle, its constable was to 'guard the earl's manors of Embleton and Stamford with his other lands and manors', an important responsibility in an age of banditry and Scottish raiding. In emergencies, the villagers might shelter with their possessions inside the castle, despite the difficulty which the castle's remote location must have caused. It has been suggested that Lancaster planned a new town in the large space south of the great gatehouse, though no trace of this has been found, and possibly the scheme was never carried out. Repairs and alterations to the castle were funded in part out of the income of the barony: from woodlands, watermills, dovecotes and the rental of farmsteads. Administrators inside the castle drew up the accounts, which also contained other buildings for the wider lordship, including a barn and a byre. Local courts continued to be held at Embleton in the Moot Hall, remodelled in 1586 but still standing today.

In 1461, for the first time, fighting came to Dunstanburgh, during the so-called Wars of the Roses, fought between the houses of Lancaster and York for possession of the English Crown. Dunstanburgh, like Alnwick, Warkworth and Bamburgh castles, came to symbolise control over the eastern borders, and kept open a route by which Lancastrians could invade from Scotland or from France. The Yorkist claimant Edward IV (1461–83) resolved to capture them, but the joint constable, Sir Ralph Percy (1425–64), held Dunstanburgh for the Lancastrians, even after the Yorkist victory at Towton in March. He only submitted to the Yorkists in September 1461.

The following year, Margaret of Anjou (1430–82), wife of the Lancastrian king Henry VI, and a French army landed from Scotland at Bamburgh, causing Percy to revert to the

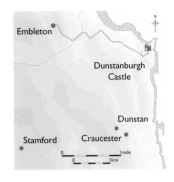

Above: *Map showing the settlements closest to Dunstanburgh. The castle lay nearly 2 miles from Embleton, the nearest manor*
Left: *Embleton dovecote, possibly medieval in date. Accounts of the 1440s mention the king's dovecote in the village among other estate buildings there*

Right: 15th-century manuscript illustration showing the earl of Warwick 'the kingmaker' at the battle of Barnet in 1471. In 1462, Warwick led the Yorkist army besieging Dunstanburgh Castle

Lancastrian cause. The Yorkist force that then besieged Dunstanburgh in December 1462 for a second time was led by the earls of Warwick and Worcester and Sir Ralph Grey; the writer Sir Thomas Malory fought under their command. Faced with starvation, Percy surrendered at Christmas. This did not mark the end of the struggle, and only in June 1464 did the Yorkists secure possession of the castle for good.

DUNSTANBURGH IN THE 16TH CENTURY

In the late 15th century Dunstanburgh Castle went into a marked decline. Though still garrisoned, it was neglected by the Crown, so much so that its occupants seem to have taken to piracy to maintain the castle's stores. In 1470 a Breton merchant complained to Edward IV that in the previous year his ship, bound for Newcastle, had been intercepted at sea; its crew were thrown into 'a derke prison in your castell of Dunstanburgh', where one of them died, and its cargo was looted.

The castle's buildings began to fall into disrepair in the 16th century, and by 1520 it was being considered as a source of building materials to repair other castles. A report of January 1514 that two missing warships bound for Scotland were found at Dunstanburgh does not provide evidence that the site was functioning as a major port, as was once believed; the vessels remained offshore, although their captain evidently landed there, perhaps at the medieval jetty south of the castle. By the 1530s Dunstanburgh Castle had become 'a very ruinous house and of small strength'; only the great gatehouse was still habitable (the constable's house was also mentioned a few years later), and there were defects to the stonework, timbers and lead roofs throughout the castle. The surveyors felt that the castle would remain useful if repairs were undertaken immediately: as a report of 1550 ran, 'surely it would be a great refuge to the inhabitants of those parts, if enemies came to annoy them, either arriving by sea or coming by land out of Scotland'. But, realistically, Dunstanburgh was not strategically sited, lying too far from the Scottish border to be of any value in defending it.

In 1594 Edmund Craster, lord of the manor of Craster, died. His widow, Alice, moved from her home at Craster Tower to Dunstanburgh and spent the three final years of her life there. She probably inhabited part of the great gatehouse, for she seems to have been responsible for narrowing the gateway in the eastern wall of John of Gaunt's mantlet. The gatehouse must have provided comfortable accommodation, for Alice Craster was evidently quite rich. She farmed the land within and around the castle, keeping 18 plough oxen, 32 cattle, 3 horses, 145 sheep and 12 pigs. At her death in 1597, furniture in her possession included a bed, 2 truckle beds, 2 tables, 2 chairs, 7 stools, 2 benches, a cupboard and a chest; other items included a silver salt cellar, 6 spoons, 18 pewter vessels, 3 trenchers, kitchen utensils, 2 spinning wheels, bed linen and table linen.

The union of the crowns of Scotland and England in 1603 with the accession of James VI of Scotland to the English throne as James I of England made the castle even more redundant, and in 1604 it was finally sold. In 1605 it passed to Sir Ralph Grey, who owned estates at nearby Howick Hall.

Below: Craster Tower, the fortified manor house of Craster, still in the private ownership of the ancient Craster family. Much of the house was rebuilt in the 18th and 19th centuries but the tower to the right survives from the 14th century

LATER HISTORY

Dunstanburgh remained with the Grey family until 1869. Under their ownership, much of the promontory was evidently used again for arable farming. An engraving made by Francis Place in 1678 shows harvest under way in the fields west of the castle, and a note added to the 1695 English translation of William Camden's *Britannia* records the quantities of wheat, barley and hay harvested inside the castle walls. At about this time, efforts were made to drain and improve the site of the northern mere, and even this boggy ground was ploughed for a time.

Francis Place's drawing, which appears to be very accurate from those details which can still be checked, is useful because it also shows architectural features that no longer survive. For example, it allows the gradual dilapidation of the western wall to be charted. Mounds of stone still lying along the foot of the castle outcrop suggest that, as was common practice elsewhere, the ruins were treated as a convenient source of good-quality building stone. Whether or not this was encouraged by the Grey family is not known.

The present village of Craster was founded by Shafto Craster in about 1780, when it was known as Craster Seahouses; then, it had only a tiny landing for fishing boats. The snug harbour was created using dynamite in 1906, to allow the export of Whinstone (basalt) slabs to supply London's streets with kerbstones. The medieval hamlet of Craucester, which lay a little further inland near Craster Tower, was finally abandoned in the 18th century.

J M W Turner was the most famous of a succession of artists who visited Dunstanburgh in the late 18th and early 19th centuries. Each attempted to capture on canvas the

Below: Sketch of Dunstanburgh Castle by Francis Place, 1678. This sketch is the only source for many details now missing, including the battlements of the great gatehouse, and the lower storey of John of Gaunt's gate

Left: Bathing house at Howick, built by the Grey family in the mid-19th century, with fine views towards the picturesque ruins of Dunstanburgh Castle. The quarries in the foreground may well have provided stone for the new castle in the 14th century

romantic decay of the ruins and the drama of their setting.

Events of the 19th and early 20th centuries leave us with some of the castle's greatest puzzles. For example, there are vague references to restorations in the early 19th century; some physical signs of this work are also recognisable. But unfortunately the restoration was largely undocumented – only a few undated drawings survive – and it was completed so skilfully that in places it remains difficult to distinguish medieval from modern masonry. The entrance to the gate-passage and the barbican, both crucial to the understanding of Thomas of Lancaster's grand design, are two of the most problematic areas. Similarly, some of the clearance work carried out in the 1920s in preparation for the bequest of the monument to the State by its last proprietor, Sir Arthur Sutherland, a Newcastle shipowner, was poorly documented by modern standards, leaving us with as many questions as answers.

Above: Prefabricated pill-box built in 1940 against the threat of enemy landings on Embleton Beach. The west face has been damaged by an explosion and rifle fire, apparently during a later training exercise
Below: The undamaged embrasure covering Nova Scotia beach

DUNSTANBURGH IN THE SECOND WORLD WAR

With the defeat of Norway by Nazi Germany in April 1940, Britain unexpectedly faced the threat of invasion on the long and poorly defended east coast. Long beaches like Embleton's, immediately to the north of Dunstanburgh Castle, were vulnerable to seaborne landings and Northumberland's countryside, with few trees or people, potentially allowed the enemy to drop airborne troops to capture targets inland, so that the landing force could advance rapidly.

To prevent this, the coast was immediately defended. A visitor to Dunstanburgh in 1940 would have seen steel structures in the sea, designed to wreck landing craft; rows of concrete cubes on the beaches to halt tanks; and triple lines of coiled barbed wire along the sea front, intended to impede infantry. Today, the small concrete gun emplacements known as pillboxes are the most obvious remains: one occupies the slope to the south of the castle. The main buildings of a top secret radar station, designed to detect low flying aircraft and fleets of ships, also survive on the crest of the escarpment between Craster and Dunstanburgh. In 1940, local people knew only that this had 'something to do with radio'.

To meet the immediate demands of the emergency at this time many historic monuments in coastal locations were refortified, sometimes brutally. But although Dunstanburgh was incorporated into the system of coastal defences, the ruins themselves escaped major changes, because they already provided good defensive positions. North of the Lilburn Tower is a 'slit trench', facing towards Embleton beach. To prevent the

Dunstanburgh in Wartime

'Digging trenches on the fine sands of Embleton beach was easier said than done'

Above: Bill Hawkins with comrades at his Company's field camp at Wooler
Below: Bill Hawkins enlisted as a 17-year-old in 1939. After Northumberland he saw action in North Africa and at Monte Cassino

In 1940, Bill Hawkins, serving with the 1st/4th Battalion Essex Regiment, was sent up to Northumberland to defend the coast:

'We did training exercises and beach defence at Embleton, right by Dunstanburgh Castle. Our platoon had to dig trenches on the beach. This was easier said than done as the sand was so fine it fell back and filled the hole you'd just dug. It wasn't very successful. When we got sandbags, that was a great advantage. It would have been hard to defend our positions if we had been attacked. All we had was rifles. The dunes behind us would have given some protection, I suppose. They have now been converted into a golf course.

'We were afraid that the Germans might land tanks on the beach. We didn't have any tanks of our own so we commandeered a bread van from Wooler and equipped it with coils of Dannert [barbed] wire, two or three picks and shovels, sandbags and a box of anti-tank Hawkins mines. We rode around on bikes, practising. Some of the chaps from London couldn't even ride a bicycle.

'There was a big spy scare. All troops and personnel were given to understand that the enemy may be active as a Fifth Column. There weren't supposed to be any lights flickering out to sea and we had to report if people didn't use their black-out curtains properly, in case they were signalling to the Germans. We always had to keep a sharp lookout. One morning, one of my chaps shouted that there was something coming in from the sea. We gave the alarm and everyone stood to – then we realised it was just the sun coming up.'

landing force breaking away quickly from the beach, long anti-tank lines were built, with ditches where rivers and other natural features could not be used. There was a risk that invaders might move southwards from Embleton beach, passing Dunstanburgh, so an anti-tank ditch was dug across the level ground between Thomas of Lancaster's water-filled moat and the steep slope of the castle outcrop. A minefield, comprising 170 mines and covered by the surviving pillbox and several slit trenches, blocked the route to the west. In low sunlight, the rows of pits where the mines were dug out after the war are visible. They were evidently easily triggered anti-personnel devices, because local people remember that an explosion one night in 1940 caused panic that the invasion had begun. The following morning, it became clear that a fox had wandered into the minefield.

CARING FOR DUNSTANBURGH TODAY

Current management of the castle and its environs by English Heritage and the National Trust continues to affect what will be handed on to future generations. The archaeological survey carried out by English Heritage in 2003 revealed that the shallow pool valued by the National Trust as a habitat for wildlife was, seven centuries ago, the site of one of the castle's ornamental lakes (see page 22). Now it is clear that the area is as valuable historically as it is environmentally, and will have to be cared for accordingly. Elsewhere, gorse has been cut back to expose medieval earthworks and limit damage by roots and burrowing rabbits. Both organisations are committed to supporting further research on which sound management decisions can be based.

Below: Occasionally, as in February 2004, the north mere floods again, giving a good impression of the castle's medieval appearance.